BACKYARD DETECTIVE

Critters Up Close

BACKYARD

DETECTIVE

Critters

Up

Close

NIC BISHOP

SCHOLASTIC PRESS ❖ NEW YORK

CONTENTS

TAKE A CLOSER LOOK

WHAT'S UNDERFOOT?

A FLOWER FEAST

EATING YOUR VEGETABLES

TOOLSHED GUESTS

THE WEED JUNGLE

A LEAFY HIDEOUT

LOOK UP!

BE A BACKYARD DETECTIVE

FIND THAT ANIMAL

TAKE A CLOSER LOOK

HOW TO USE THIS BOOK

Something exciting is going on right under your nose. Right in your backyard, tiny critters are crawling, flying, hiding, prowling, eating—and getting eaten. This fascinating miniworld is yours to discover, if you take a closer look. In this book, you can find more than 125 bugs, insects, and other small animals going about their lives. Each one has a favorite place, or habitat, where it likes to live. It might be in the soil, under a log, or in the trees. Study the seven life-size images of backyard habitats and see how many critters you can spy. Some are masters of camouflage and are hard to find. Others are bold and flashy. Each habitat image shows, in true-to-life size, how the animals really look and interact in the wild. Try to guess their names and what they are up to. Then use the field notes that follow to check your guesses. And search your own backyard for these animals.

The more carefully you look, the more you'll discover. You may need to take a magnifying glass on your backyard expeditions. In this book, the magnifying glass shows

September 20

9 a.m. Sunny morning. Saw white butterfly on cabbages in vegetable patch.

2 inches

black spots

1 inch

yellow

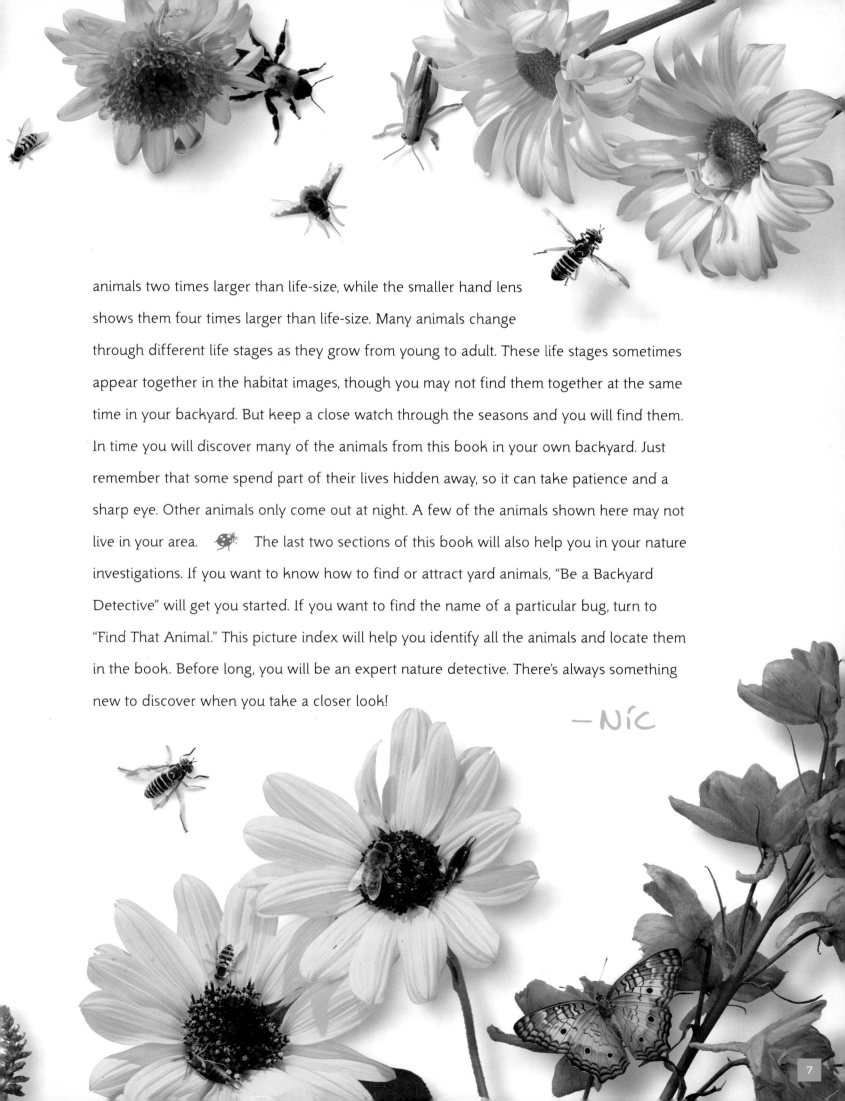

animals two times larger than life-size, while the smaller hand lens

shows them four times larger than life-size. Many animals change

through different life stages as they grow from young to adult. These life stages sometimes

appear together in the habitat images, though you may not find them together at the same

time in your backyard. But keep a close watch through the seasons and you will find them.

In time you will discover many of the animals from this book in your own backyard. Just

remember that some spend part of their lives hidden away, so it can take patience and a

sharp eye. Other animals only come out at night. A few of the animals shown here may not

live in your area.   The last two sections of this book will also help you in your nature

investigations. If you want to know how to find or attract yard animals, "Be a Backyard

Detective" will get you started. If you want to find the name of a particular bug, turn to

"Find That Animal." This picture index will help you identify all the animals and locate them

in the book. Before long, you will be an expert nature detective. There's always something

new to discover when you take a closer look!

—Nic

WHAT'S UNDERFOOT?

skink

pseudoscorpion

The soil is a great place for a critter hunt. Look under a log. Turn over the leaf litter. It's crawling with sow bugs and worms, ants and millipedes. These are nature's recyclers. They chomp through the dead things that fall onto the ground, chewing them to smaller and smaller bits till they become part of the soil again. These recyclers have an important job. Imagine the mountains of leaves and sticks that would pile up if they were not broken down. You'll need a magnifying glass to see the smallest litter eaters. Look carefully for **springtails**. They have forked tails that can flip them into the air. You may spot **red mites** feeding on rotting plant juices. Some mites are predators, eating other animals. The **pseudoscorpion** is the strangest mini-predator you'll see. It grabs prey with big pincers and kills it with a poison bite. If you find **worm casts** on the ground, it's a sure sign of **earthworms** at work. Thousands live under your yard, burrowing through the earth. They swallow dirt, taking in nutrients and excreting the rest. Worm casts are the squiggly soil droppings they sometimes leave aboveground. Earthworms are easiest to find at night, when they come to the surface. Take a flashlight and you might see one slip out of its burrow to grab a dead leaf to eat. Other litter eaters come out at night, too. They have bodies that would dry out in the sun during the day. Look for **millipedes** and **sow bugs**, nibbling fallen leaves and branches. Both these animals can ooze a smelly liquid to keep predators from eating them. **Earwigs** eat plants and chew holes in flower petals. Many predators are busy at night. **Centipedes** have thin bodies to sneak through cracks in the litter. They catch prey with poison pincers. The **thread centipede** can

springtail

red mites

millipede

worm cast

earthworm

earwig

centipede

sow bug

thread centipede

The animals you see here may be larger or smaller than life-size.

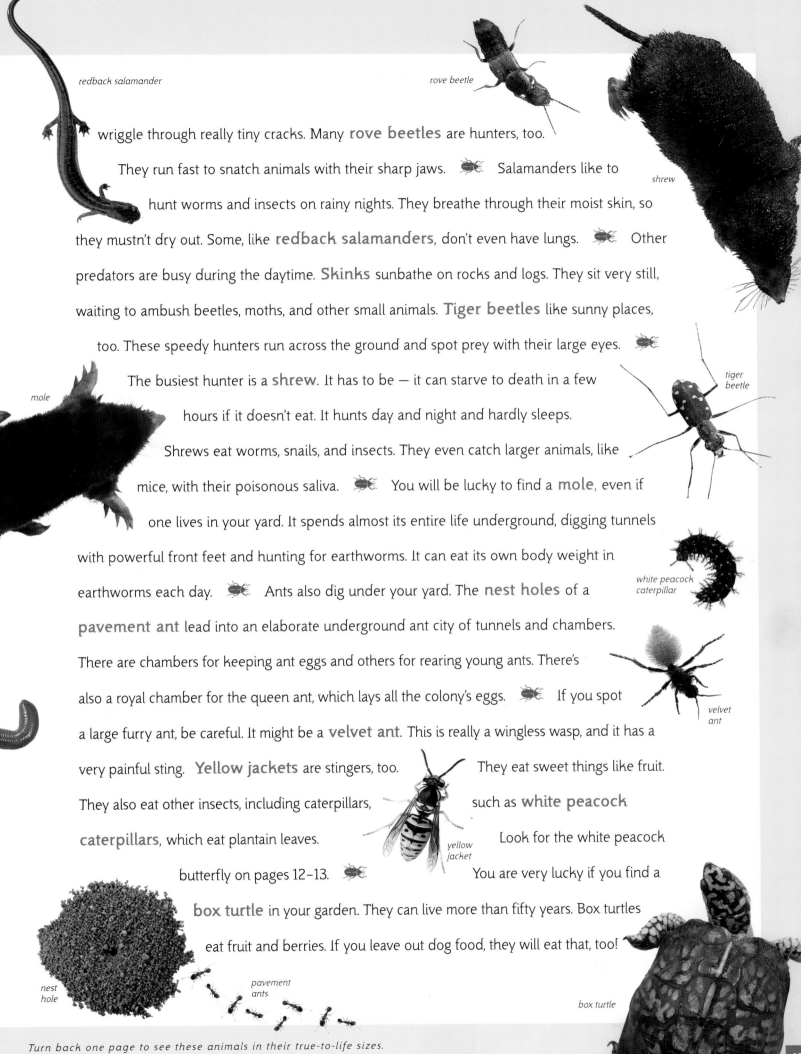

redback salamander

rove beetle

shrew

wriggle through really tiny cracks. Many **rove beetles** are hunters, too. They run fast to snatch animals with their sharp jaws. Salamanders like to hunt worms and insects on rainy nights. They breathe through their moist skin, so they mustn't dry out. Some, like **redback salamanders**, don't even have lungs. Other predators are busy during the daytime. **Skinks** sunbathe on rocks and logs. They sit very still, waiting to ambush beetles, moths, and other small animals. **Tiger beetles** like sunny places, too. These speedy hunters run across the ground and spot prey with their large eyes. The busiest hunter is a **shrew**. It has to be — it can starve to death in a few hours if it doesn't eat. It hunts day and night and hardly sleeps. Shrews eat worms, snails, and insects. They even catch larger animals, like mice, with their poisonous saliva. You will be lucky to find a **mole**, even if one lives in your yard. It spends almost its entire life underground, digging tunnels with powerful front feet and hunting for earthworms. It can eat its own body weight in earthworms each day. Ants also dig under your yard. The **nest holes** of a **pavement ant** lead into an elaborate underground ant city of tunnels and chambers. There are chambers for keeping ant eggs and others for rearing young ants. There's also a royal chamber for the queen ant, which lays all the colony's eggs. If you spot a large furry ant, be careful. It might be a **velvet ant**. This is really a wingless wasp, and it has a very painful sting. **Yellow jackets** are stingers, too. They eat sweet things like fruit. They also eat other insects, including caterpillars, such as **white peacock caterpillars**, which eat plantain leaves. Look for the white peacock butterfly on pages 12–13. You are very lucky if you find a **box turtle** in your garden. They can live more than fifty years. Box turtles eat fruit and berries. If you leave out dog food, they will eat that, too!

mole

tiger beetle

white peacock caterpillar

velvet ant

yellow jacket

nest hole

pavement ants

box turtle

Turn back one page to see these animals in their true-to-life sizes.

white
peacock
butterfly

A FLOWER FEAST

honeybee

o us, flowers are pretty. To insects, they are food. Watch a **honeybee** when it visits a flower. It reaches in with a long tongue to lap up a sugary energy drink called nectar. Insects need lots of energy to fly, so nectar is great food for them. The honeybee stores some of the nectar in a special stomach called a honey crop. It also gathers yellow grains, called pollen, from the flower. Then it carries the nectar and pollen to its nest, or hive, where it is fed to young bees. Some of the nectar is passed to other bees, which turn it into honey and store it for the winter. Each flower makes the tiniest amount of nectar at a time, so insect visitors work hard to gather enough to keep going. Honeybees have to visit more than 20,000 flowers to collect enough nectar to make just one teaspoon of honey! Try following a **bumblebee** around the flower bed. It stops for only a

bumblebee

few seconds at one flower before moving to the next. When it feeds, the bumblebee collects nectar and pollen for its young, just as a honeybee does. When loaded with supplies, it may weigh twice as much as normal. Yet it easily flies one mile or so back to its nest. Butterflies, like **Baltimores**,

Baltimore
butterfly

fritillaries, and **white peacocks**, can taste sweet nectar with their feet. As soon as they land on a flower, they uncurl a long feeding tube, called a proboscis, to suck up their food. Some moths also visit the flower bed. The

fritillary
butterfly

hummingbird clearwing moth can zip from bloom to bloom without needing to land. It has an especially long proboscis, so it can sip from each flower while it hovers nearby. Wasps are nectar drinkers, too.

hummingbird
clearwing
moth

The animals you see here may be larger or smaller than life-size.

paper wasp

thread-waisted wasp

Paper wasps and **thread-waisted wasps** hunt insects to feed to their young, but they have to stop at the flower bed for a drink of flight fuel. 🦋 Flowers don't make nectar and pollen just to feed hungry insects. They need insect visitors to help them make seeds. When an insect stops at a flower, some pollen grains stick to its body. Only when the insect visits another flower of the same type, and some of this pollen falls onto female parts of the flower, can that plant make seeds. This is a very important relationship. Without insects many plants would eventually disappear, and without flowers many insects would starve. 🦋 Flower visitors have to watch out for predators. A **Mydas fly** may be lurking nearby, and it can fly fast to catch a bee or a fly. A **crab spider** may be crouching inside a flower, ready to grab an insect with its front legs. Some crab spiders can even change color to match their flower. Look for the same spider in the weed patch on pages 24 – 25. The **bee fly** has a really sneaky way of going after prey. It watches for bees visiting flowers. Then it follows one back to the nest. The bee fly lays its eggs near the bees' nest. When they hatch, the bee fly's larvae enter the bees' nest to eat the bee larvae. 🦋

Mydas fly

crab spider

bee fly

Most animals — and people, too — are afraid of bees because they can sting. But you don't have to be afraid of a **drone fly**. It looks like a honeybee and even buzzes like a honeybee. But it can't sting. It's mimicking or pretending to be a bee so that other animals will leave it alone. Being a mimic is a great way to fool other animals into thinking that you are dangerous. Many different **hover flies** have black and yellow stripes and look like wasps, but they can't sting. They are pretending, too.

drone fly

hover flies

Turn back one page to see these animals in their true-to-life sizes.

hornworm
caterpillar

EATING YOUR VEGETABLES

It's fun to eat fresh vegetables from your garden. That's if hungry insects haven't got there first. Look closely and you'll find dozens of small creatures thriving in your vegetable garden. The hornworm caterpillar loves to feed on tomato leaves. A baby caterpillar will increase 5,000 times in size by the time it's full-grown.

open
hornworm
pupa case

hornworm
moth eggs

baby
hornworm
caterpillars

Then it crawls to the ground and digs a burrow. The caterpillar turns into a dark brown pupa. During this resting stage, the pupa does not move, but some amazing things happen inside. The caterpillar body breaks down as wings, legs, and antennae grow. Eventually, the pupa splits open, and an adult hornworm moth crawls out. Look for this moth on page 48. The moth looks completely different from the caterpillar. Soon it is ready to lay eggs on more of your tomato plants. The cabbage white butterfly visits your vegetable garden to look for cabbages to lay eggs on. A butterfly can taste with its feet, so it recognizes the right plant as soon as it lands. In a few days, cabbage white caterpillars will be eating your cabbages!

cabbage
white butterfly
eggs

cabbage
white
caterpillar

cabbage
white
butterfly

Many insects eat only their favorite food plants. A cabbage white caterpillar won't eat tomato leaves. A hornworm caterpillar won't eat cabbage leaves. The Colorado potato beetle likes potato leaves, and the striped cucumber beetle likes cucumber and squash leaves. So you will usually find them on these plants. Other insects are less fussy. The Japanese beetle and spotted cucumber beetle eat lots of different plants. You might find them anywhere in the garden. Some plant

Colorado
potato beetle

striped
cucumber beetle

spotted
cucumber beetle

Japanese beetle

The animals you see here may be larger or smaller than life-size.

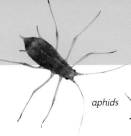
aphids

green stinkbug

squash bug

eaters don't eat leaves. They suck plant juice instead. Squash bugs and green stinkbugs have a sharp tube mouth, like a drinking straw. They stab this into plants to suck out the juice, or sap. Both these bugs can repel predators by making a bad smell, just as a skunk does.

Some of the smallest sapsuckers in your yard are aphids. Look for them on young stems and buds. Often there are so many that they harm the plant. Where you find pesky aphids, you may find ladybug beetles nearby. An adult ladybug can eat fifty aphids in one day. It

ladybug larva

stabs them with sharp jaws and sucks out their body juices. Ladybug larvae eat aphids, too, so people like to see them in the garden.

bean beetle

When in danger, a ladybug can ooze bad-tasting orange blood from its

bean beetle eggs

knees. Not all ladybugs are gardeners' friends. The bean beetle is a type of ladybug that eats bean plants. Look for its yellow eggs on the underside of bean leaves. One bean beetle can lay 1,000 eggs in its life! They hatch into hungry yellow larvae. Look for a green grass snake. It hunts grasshoppers and crickets. Some snakes have venom and are dangerous, but this one will not hurt

bean beetle larva

you. Snakes are so shy that you are lucky to see them at all. The leopard frog might

green grass snake

visit your garden at night, hunting for spiders, worms, and crickets. It's an amazing hopper and can leap 6 feet in one hop. Night is a good time to watch other critters eating your vegetables. The garden snail hides under stones or logs during the day. At night, it glides on a trail

garden snail

of slime dribbled from the underside of its body. Its feelers are sensitive to touch and taste, and they have a small eye on each tip. If it finds a tasty plant, a snail eats with the hundreds of tiny teeth on its tongue. When it senses danger, the snail pulls its feelers and body inside its shell.

A slug is a type of snail that doesn't have a shell. Most slugs like to eat plants. But the large leopard slug eats all sorts of things, sometimes even other slugs!

leopard slug

leopard frog

Turn back one page to see these animals in their true-to-life sizes.

Beets

SAVER

PARS

BEANS
BEETS

INS

21

TOOLSHED GUESTS

house mouse

You may not notice them, but critters are living in your toolshed. As soon as the sun starts to set, things get busy. Mice scamper on benches. Crickets chirp from dark corners, and geckos hunt for insects. Some of these shed guests may live in your house, too. Most shed guests are not particular about food. A **house mouse** will eat candles, or even soap. But it loves the birdseed you store in the toolshed. It also likes a cozy hideaway to rear its **babies**. The inside of an old tin can may do.

house mouse babies

You may have **white-footed mice** in your shed if you live in the countryside. Like house mice, they find their way in the dark with sensitive whiskers and a good sense of smell. They also have keen ears and scamper off when they hear you coming.

white-footed mouse

American cockroach

Cockroaches will eat clothing, wood, or even shoe polish. Their flattened bodies help them hide in cracks during the day. At night, they wave long feelers around to sense for enemies like house mice, which enjoy a meal of cockroach. If it stays out of trouble, the **German cockroach** may live for about five months, and the bigger **American cockroach** can live for two years. Look for **cockroach egg capsules**, shaped like little purses. Cockroaches are masters of escape. Special feelers at the back warn them of sudden air movements. So if you try to sneak up behind one, it will run for

German cockroach

cockroach egg capsules

the nearest crack. Cockroaches are one of the most successful insects to have ever lived. Fossils show they were scuttling around even before there were dinosaurs. **Silverfish** have been around even longer. Scientists believe they are one of the oldest types of insect on Earth.

silverfish

Look for them inside books. They hide between the pages and nibble the glues and starches used to make books. They also like flour

The animals you see here may be larger or smaller than life-size.

house fly

house fly pupae

house fly squeezing out of pupa case

and bread crumbs. **House flies** love garbage. They lay eggs on rotting food, and the fly maggots, shown on page 48, start munching as soon as they hatch. After a week, each maggot turns into a **pupa**. The pupa splits open a few days later and the **fly squeezes out**. A fly may live for a month, if it isn't eaten first. **House spiders** hang sticky webs to trap them. **Jumping spiders** sneak up and pounce on them. Jumping spiders have good

house spider

eyesight and check out everything that moves. When two meet, they signal each other by waving their legs. Otherwise, one might mistake the other for a meal! **House geckos** catch flies, too. Geckos can climb walls and even ceilings after prey. Their toes have special pads covered in tiny suction cups. They especially enjoy juicy **house crickets**. House crickets aren't much of a pest in the shed, but they do make a lot of noise. The male cricket chirps by rubbing its wings together. Female crickets listen with ears on their front legs.

jumping spiders

The ants you find are probably looking for food scraps. Black **Formica ants** eat almost anything, but they love sweet things. When an ant finds food, it uses a special liquid from its body to lay a scent trail for other ants to follow. If you see some really big ants, watch out. These are young **queen carpenter ants**. They have just left their mother's nest and are looking for a place to start their own nest. Carpenter ants make a nest by chewing tunnels in wood, and the timber of your toolshed will do just fine. Young queen ants have **wings** when they first fly from their old nest. They lose their wings before they start digging a new home. Look out for **paper wasps**, too. In the spring, queen paper wasps look for a nice dry place to build their nests. By summer, you may have hundreds of wasps buzzing in and out of your toolshed.

queen carpenter ant

winged queen carpenter ant

house cricket

Formica ant

paper wasp

house gecko

Turn back one page to see these animals in their true-to-life sizes.

THE WEED JUNGLE

crab
spider

If you have a weed patch in your yard, don't pull it out. Take a nature expedition there instead. Your weed patch is like a mini-jungle, filled with animals. Each is looking for something to eat, or trying to avoid being eaten. The **green grass snake** slides between grass stems, looking for **grasshoppers**. **Ladybug beetles** wander up and down leaves, eating plump aphids. The **crab spider** sits

grasshopper

ladybug
beetle

harvestman
(or daddy
longlegs)

quietly on a flower, waiting to ambush prey. The **nursery web spider** is another hunter. When it feels the vibration of an insect moving nearby, it pounces. You might think the **harvestman**, or **daddy longlegs**, is a spider, too, but it's not. It has eight legs like a spider, but it does not make silk or have poison fangs. It eats dead things

nursery
web spider

painted lady
butterfly
eggs

painted lady
caterpillar

and preys on small insects. The weed patch is also an important butterfly nursery. Look for **painted lady butterfly eggs** and **caterpillars** on mallow and thistle weeds. When they are ready, each caterpillar crawls to a neighboring plant to turn into a **pupa**. Ten days later, the pupa splits open and the **butterfly crawls out**. It dries its new wings in the sun and flies off. Watch for **butterflies** returning to lay their eggs.

painted
lady pupa

monarch
pupa

You may find **monarch caterpillars** in the weed patch, munching milkweed plants. The caterpillar's black and yellow stripes are a warning that it's poisonous.

painted lady
butterfly
crawling out

Milkweed plants are toxic, but instead of being hurt, the caterpillar safely stores the milkweed's poisons in its body. Then, if a bird tries to eat the caterpillar, it gets very sick and learns to stay away from those black and yellow stripes. The **monarch pupa** is also protected by milkweed poisons in its body. So is the **butterfly**. Animals learn to leave

monarch
caterpillar

painted lady
butterfly

monarch butterfly

The animals you see here may be larger or smaller than life-size.

milkweed bug

hairstreak butterfly

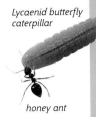
Lycaenid butterfly caterpillar

honey ant

milkweed bugs alone, too. They eat milkweeds and are poisonous, just like the monarch. Their bright colors mean, "I taste bad!" The hairstreak butterfly isn't poisonous, but it has a neat way to trick predators. Two tails on its back wings look like a head with antennae. When a predator attacks the wrong end, the butterfly takes off to safety. Some Lycaenid butterfly caterpillars use a different way to defend themselves.

honey ant

They have bodyguards. The caterpillar eats clover plants and oozes a sweet liquid called honeydew from its back. Ants, like the honey ant, love sweet liquids and follow the caterpillar around to drink the honeydew. In return, they guard the caterpillar from other insects. A young spittlebug protects itself by blowing bubbles. It sucks plant juice for food and blows air into a liquid it oozes from its body to make a frothy home to hide in. The adult spittlebug, called a froghopper, no longer makes bubbles. It protects itself by jumping from predators with a powerful leap. The scarlet and green leafhopper is another super-leaper. Lots of different animals visit the weed patch. Dragonflies, like the blue dasher, zoom in from nearby ponds to catch insects in their front legs. Weed flowers hum

spittlebug

froghoppers

with the sound of locust borer beetles, honeybees,

locust borer beetle

green sweat bees, and nectar and pollen. The great

scarlet and green leafhopper

mining bees, busily gathering golden digger wasp takes nectar, katydids and crickets to feed its young.

honeybee

too, but it hunts the weeds for On warm summer

afternoons, you will hear crickets singing in your weed patch. Male tree crickets make a soft trilling sound, to court female crickets. If a female likes the male, she nudges him to stop singing, so he won't attract any other females — or predators. The more

tree cricket

great golden digger wasp

you look and listen, the more you'll learn about nature from the

weed jungle. It's one of the most interesting parts of the yard.

green sweat bee

mining bee

blue dasher

Turn back one page to see these animals in their true-to-life sizes.

young katydid

anole

A LEAFY HIDEOUT

Go leaf peeping. Lots of interesting animals live in the bushes and trees around your yard, but you have to look carefully to find them. Many are camouflage experts. The green **katydid** matches the color of its leafy background, so predators like the **anole** can't see it. Being green helps the anole hide, too, from predators like cats and birds. **Treehoppers** have another way to hide. They look like thorns, which no animal likes to tangle with. If a predator does see one, the treehopper has another trick. It vanishes with a sudden leap. Brown **cicadas** are hard to spot on a tree trunk, but you'll have no problem hearing them. Their shrill buzzing is the loudest insect noise in your yard. A cicada spends its early life underground, as a nymph feeding on roots. After a few years, the nymph climbs up a tree, its skin splits, and the adult crawls out. Look for the empty **nymph skins** in July and August. The green **praying mantis** is also good at hiding from predators — and from the animals it wants to catch. If a **blow fly** lands nearby, the mantis scoops it up in its large forearms and eats everything except the wings and legs. A female mantis lays her **egg case** on a tree trunk or fence rail in the fall. The **young** hatch in spring and start catching small midges and flies right away. Lots of other predators hunt among the leaves. **Ladybugs** look for aphids and scale insects. So do **lacewings**. The **jumping spider** stalks prey like a cat. It crawls over and under leaves, looking for insects. Then it sneaks up and pounces with a huge jump. A jumping spider can

treehopper

young
praying
mantis

cicada

nymph
skin

blue bottle
blow fly

praying
mantis

green
bottle
blow fly

ladybug

praying mantis
egg case

lacewing

jumping
spider

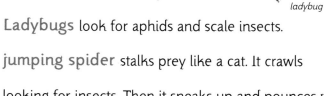

The animals you see here may be larger or smaller than life-size.

paper wasp

crane fly

young cecropia caterpillars

leap ten times its body length. The paper wasp might be hunting insects, too. Or it could be collecting wood. Paper wasps chew bits of wood and mix it with sticky saliva to make paper, which they use to build their nests. There are several types of paper wasp — you can find a different one on pages 12 – 13. Don't worry if you spot something that looks like a giant mosquito in the bushes. It's probably a crane fly, and they don't bite. The adults don't even feed. They did their eating and growing when they were larvae, living mostly on rotting plants. If you find leaf holes when you are leaf peeping, that's a clue that leaf eaters have been at work. It could be a cecropia moth caterpillar. A young cecropia caterpillar changes color as it grows. In the fall, it spins a papery cocoon in the branches and rests through the winter. The moth hatches in late spring and you may see one flying at night near your porch light. It lays eggs on leaves of maple, birch, and ash trees. You can find a cecropia moth on page 48. If a tiger swallowtail butterfly visits your yard, it may be looking for the right tree to lay its eggs on. The caterpillars eat leaves of poplar, birch, and wild cherry trees. Katydids are leaf eaters, too. In spring, you will find young katydids, which don't yet have wings as adults do.

cecropia moth caterpillar

cecropia eggs

cecropia cocoon

young katydid

On summer evenings, you can hear adult male katydids singing by rubbing their wings together. They make a soft chirping to attract adult female katydids such as the one on pages 32 – 33. Toads, frogs, and crickets also sing at night. It's a great way to stay in touch after dark. Each type of animal has a special call so that it can recognize its own kind. A green tree frog sounds like a little bell, *queenk, queenk, queenk.* Other tree frogs sound as if they are whistling, barking, or even snoring. If you spot a light winking in the dark, that's a firefly calling to other fireflies. The male firefly flashes a special signal. When a female recognizes it, she flashes her own light to tell him where she is.

green tree frog

firefly

tiger swallowtail butterfly

Turn back one page to see these animals in their true-to-life sizes.

clouded
sulfur
butterfly

damselfly

Look up!

Lie on your back and watch the sky. It's a busy place. Butterflies and beetles, wasps and flies, zoom back and forth in the sunlight. Some are looking for food. Some are looking for a place to lay their eggs. Others are escaping danger. Insects are amazing aerial acrobats. Many fly like little helicopters. As their wings beat, air is pushed down and the insect is pushed up. The yellow jacket and the paper wasp fly like this. So does the damselfly. A damselfly can hover like a helicopter and even fly backward. The large wings of a butterfly work a little differently. They make tiny whirlpools of air that help push and tug it along. Watch a clouded sulfur butterfly in the sky and see how its body bobs up and down as it flies. Insect wings move very fast. The buzzing of a bumblebee is the sound of its wings flapping 200 times each second. The whining of a mosquito in your ear is its wings beating 600 times a second. That's 36,000 flaps a minute! Insect wings are incredibly durable, so that they don't wear out. They are made of chitin, the same tough stuff an insect's body is covered with. Insect wing muscles also work incredibly hard. They are thirty times more powerful than your muscles. Dragonflies, such as the blue dasher and the widow skimmer, are the fastest flyers in your garden. Some dragonflies can reach speeds of 30 miles an hour. They are also expert at catching other creatures in the air. Their large round eyes see in all directions at once, and special hairs on a dragonfly's body can

yellow
jacket

paper
wasp

bumblebee

mosquito

blue dasher

widow
skimmer

The animals you see here may be larger or smaller than life-size.

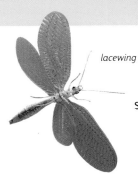
lacewing

katydid

sense how fast it's flying and which direction it's turning. Another garden flyer, the lacewing, can even hear with the hairs on its wings.

Takeoff can be tricky for an insect because it has to leap into the air before it starts beating its wings. The katydid can jump on long legs while it opens its wings, but the ladybug beetle is a lot clumsier. First it has to lift up its bright red wing covers. Then it uncurls its wings, folded like little sails underneath. Finally, it leaps with its tiny legs and starts flapping. But the ladybug doesn't always manage to open out its

ladybug beetle

wings in time, and instead of flying, it tumbles to the ground. Ladybugs are not much better at landing. They often just crash into things, but their bodies are so strong that it doesn't matter. Flies are much better at landing. They can even land upside down on a leaf. But they still have to be careful. A lynx spider may feel the vibration and

lynx spider

pounce — that's if the fly doesn't zoom off again first. Flies are very good at spotting sudden movements, and they have super-fast reflexes. Try swatting a

blow fly (blue bottle)

blow fly and see how it zips out of the way. Its tiny brain can work more quickly than yours can. Some insects fly amazing distances. If a monarch butterfly visits your garden in the fall, it may be on a 2,000-mile-long migration to Mexico where it spends the winter. Some painted lady butterflies also migrate in search of food. They can fly for hundreds of miles. A butterfly or bee flying across your yard is really a wonderful sight. Each twist and turn looks so effortless, but in fact it's very complicated. Scientists have only recently begun to discover the secrets of insect flight. And they still have a lot more to learn.

monarch butterfly

painted lady butterfly

Turn back one page to see these animals in their true-to-life sizes.

BE A BACKYARD DETECTIVE

HINTS AND PROJECTS

Exploring your yard is a great way to learn about nature. Every corner has a special community of critters waiting for you to study. In time, you will probably find many of the animals in this book. You will see other animals, too, and make many discoveries of your own. Here are some ideas to help you enjoy your backyard zoo.

Turn your yard into a nature reserve. There are many ways you can make your yard more animal-friendly. One way is to let one corner of your yard grow wild. Choose a spot with lots of bushes or other cover, and let fallen leaves and sticks accumulate. The sheltered corner will become a sanctuary for small animals. The layers of moist dead leaves will make a home for litter animals. If you put an old log in your wild corner, sow bugs and other wood eaters will move in. 🐞 If you don't have many bushes in your yard, try a wild weed patch instead. Let long grass and wildflowers overtake a sunny corner of your yard, and then go exploring for grasshoppers, caterpillars, and spiders. 🐞 Another idea is to plant a butterfly garden. Look for books to help you choose the best flowering plants for attracting butterflies. Then find a sunny spot to plant them. Buddleia is a great choice. Many people call it the "butterfly bush." Lavender, lilac, aster, goldenrod, impatiens, and bee balm are also good. Once the neighborhood butterflies know about your flowers, they will visit again and again. 🐞 You can also ask an adult to help put up a bird feeder. It may take a week or two for the birds to discover their new food. But once they do, you can go bird-watching every day.

Become a yard detective. Here are some tricks for finding insects and other small animals in the yard. Remember that most yard critters like to hide. So when you go hunting in your vegetable garden, weed patch, or bushes, look carefully on the underside of leaves. Try looking inside flowers and between clusters of leaves. Look for clues, like holes chewed in leaves or silk strands left by spiders. To find litter critters, gently turn over dead leaves. Look under logs and stones to find what's hiding underneath. But always remember to return things as you found them. You don't want to destroy the animals' homes.  You can also collect a small amount of leaf litter and soil in a bucket. Then, one bit at a time, scatter it onto a large piece of white cardboard. Use a paintbrush or small stick to gently spread out the soil and litter, and look closely for small soil animals hiding there. Remember to return the soil and litter to where it came from before it dries out. Try leaving the porch light on for a few hours during warm summer nights. If you are lucky, moths, beetles, katydids, and other insects will be attracted to the light. It's especially good to try this after a rain shower. Also make a visit to your favorite yard spots at night to see what your insect friends are up to. You may make some new discoveries. Lots of yard animals only come out at after dark.

Create a nature detective kit. Once you know some places to find animals, go back to spy on them. But take a nature detective kit with you. Your detective kit should include a magnifying glass. Take a large collecting jar, in case you want to keep a worm or other small animal a short while for a closer look. Carry a small paintbrush to gently move an insect if you need to. Remember that you should never pick up an animal by hand. You could hurt it. Or it might sting or bite you. 🐞 The most important item in your detective kit is a notebook. This will be your yard journal. Write down the date that you find an interesting animal. Record what it was doing. What was it eating? Draw a yard map to show where you found it. Then try drawing the animal and write down some facts. What color is it? How big is it? Does it have wings and legs?

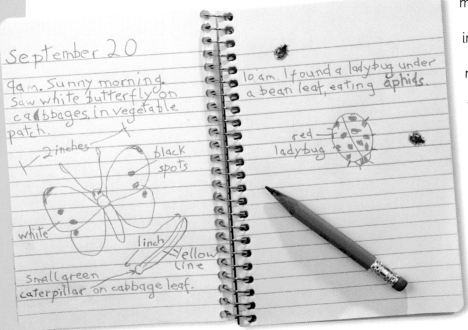

How many? Does it have antennae? These are all clues that will help you identify it later. 🐞 If you often find the same animal, adopt it as a yard friend. Write in your journal what it is doing in the yard each day. Does it change shape or color as it grows? Note if it moves to a new home. Look for eggs or young nearby. What happens to its young? Soon you'll have a better understanding about the animals you share your yard with and how they live.

Keep a yard pet. Knowing how an animal lives will help you keep one indoors to study for a few days. But always check with an adult before bringing garden critters indoors. Some are very difficult to look after. 🐞 First you will need to get a home ready for your yard pet. Use a clear jar or box with a lid that has

small air holes, so your pet cannot escape. Put some

damp moss or sand in the bottom, because

small animals get dry very easily. Then put in

some sticks and fresh leaves so your pet

has a place to climb and rest. Only keep

one pet in each home, and never leave

the container in the sun. Snails,

slugs, grasshoppers, and katydids

make good yard pets. Feed them leaves

from the same plant you found them on, or try

washed lettuce or bits of apple. Replace the uneaten food each day. A jumping spider

or a praying mantis is another good choice. They both like to eat flies. The praying mantis will

also eat small moths and grasshoppers. After three or four days, return your pet to

where you found it. Animals always prefer their own homes.

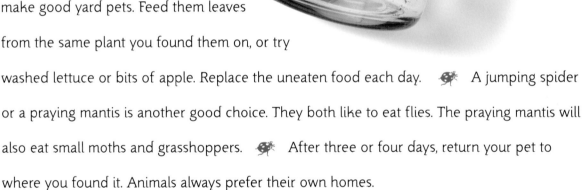

Safety First

*While the backyard makes a great place to explore nature, there are some
commonsense rules you should follow.*

1. Tell an adult before you go on a yard expedition.

2. Never hold an animal by hand unless an adult says it's okay. You may hurt the animal, or it may
nip or sting you.

3. Always be careful near wasps, bees, and ants, and never go near their nests. These insects can sting
or bite if they feel threatened, and stings can be serious for people who have allergies to them.

4. Never approach an injured or sick animal. You may frighten the animal, or it may act unpredictably
if it doesn't feel well. Sick animals can sometimes pass their diseases to humans. It's always best to
find an adult who knows how to help the animal.

FIND THAT ANIMAL

A PICTURE INDEX

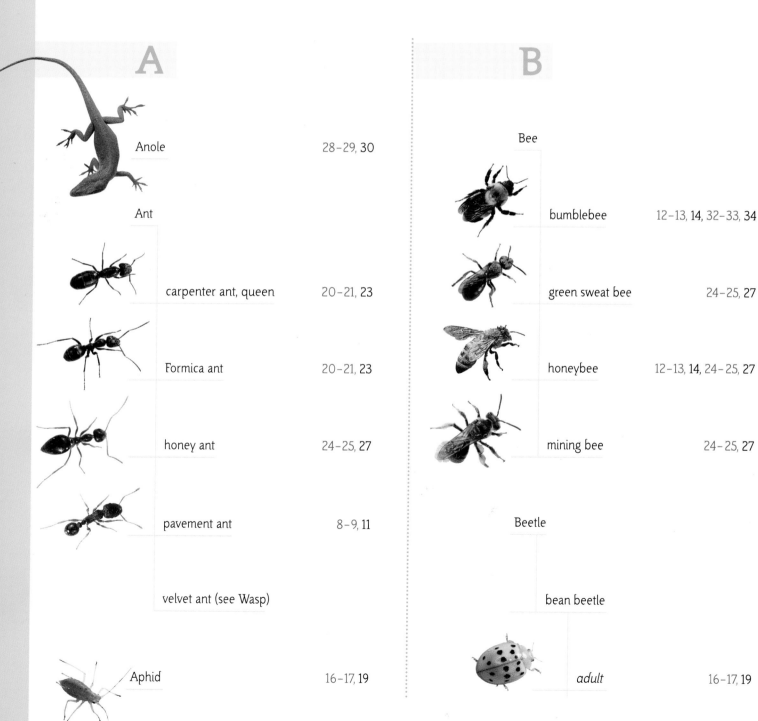

A

Anole	28–29, 30
Ant	
carpenter ant, queen	20–21, 23
Formica ant	20–21, 23
honey ant	24–25, 27
pavement ant	8–9, 11
velvet ant (see Wasp)	
Aphid	16–17, 19

B

Bee	
bumblebee	12–13, 14, 32–33, 34
green sweat bee	24–25, 27
honeybee	12–13, 14, 24–25, 27
mining bee	24–25, 27
Beetle	
bean beetle	
adult	16–17, 19

Page numbers in purple refer to pictures. Page numbers in black refer to text.

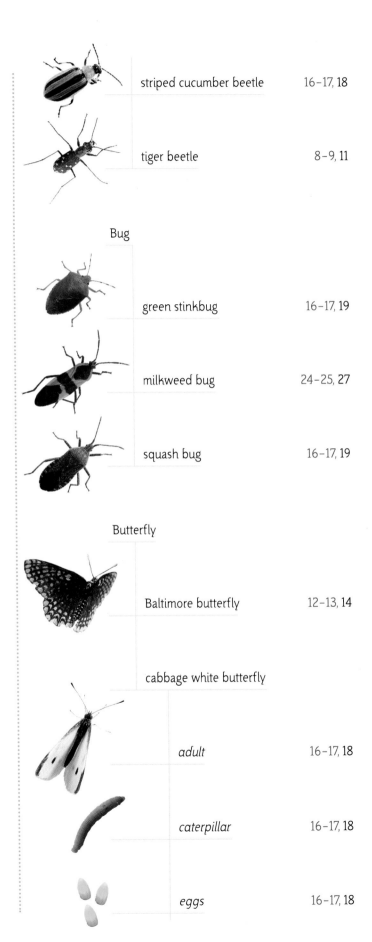

eggs 16–17, 19

larva 16–17, 19

Colorado potato beetle 16–17, 18

firefly 28–29, 31

Japanese beetle 16–17, 18

ladybug beetle

adult 16–17, 19, 24–25, 26, 32–33, 35

adult (another type) 28–29, 30

larva 16–17, 19

locust borer beetle 24–25, 27

rove beetle 8–9, 11

spotted cucumber beetle 16–17, 18

striped cucumber beetle 16–17, 18

tiger beetle 8–9, 11

Bug

green stinkbug 16–17, 19

milkweed bug 24–25, 27

squash bug 16–17, 19

Butterfly

Baltimore butterfly 12–13, 14

cabbage white butterfly

adult 16–17, 18

caterpillar 16–17, 18

eggs 16–17, 18

41

Page numbers in purple refer to pictures. Page numbers in **black** refer to text.

*Page numbers in purple refer to pictures. Page numbers in **black** refer to text.*

Cockroach

American cockroach

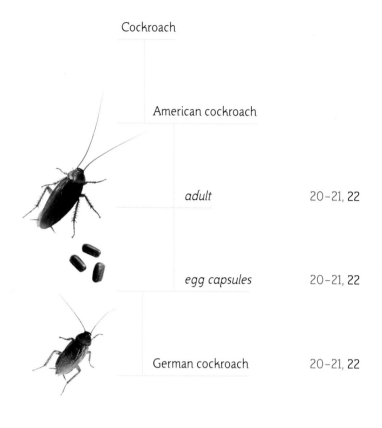

Cricket

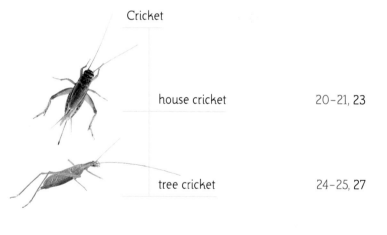

D

Daddy Longlegs (see Harvestman)

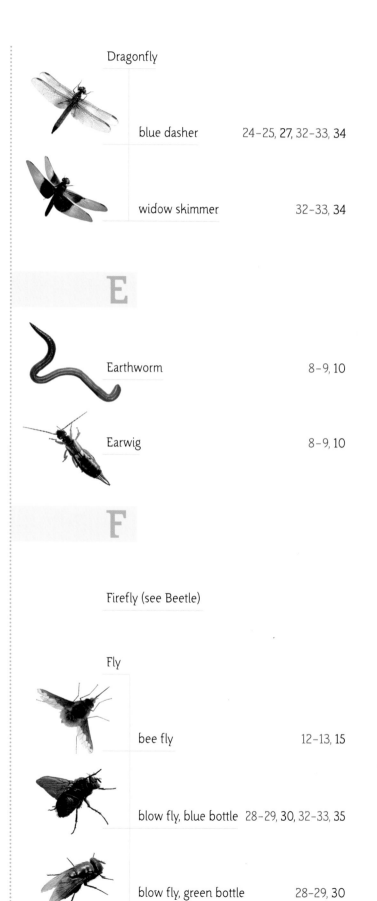

Dragonfly

E

F

Firefly (see Beetle)

Fly

*Page numbers in purple refer to pictures. Page numbers in **black** refer to text.*

43

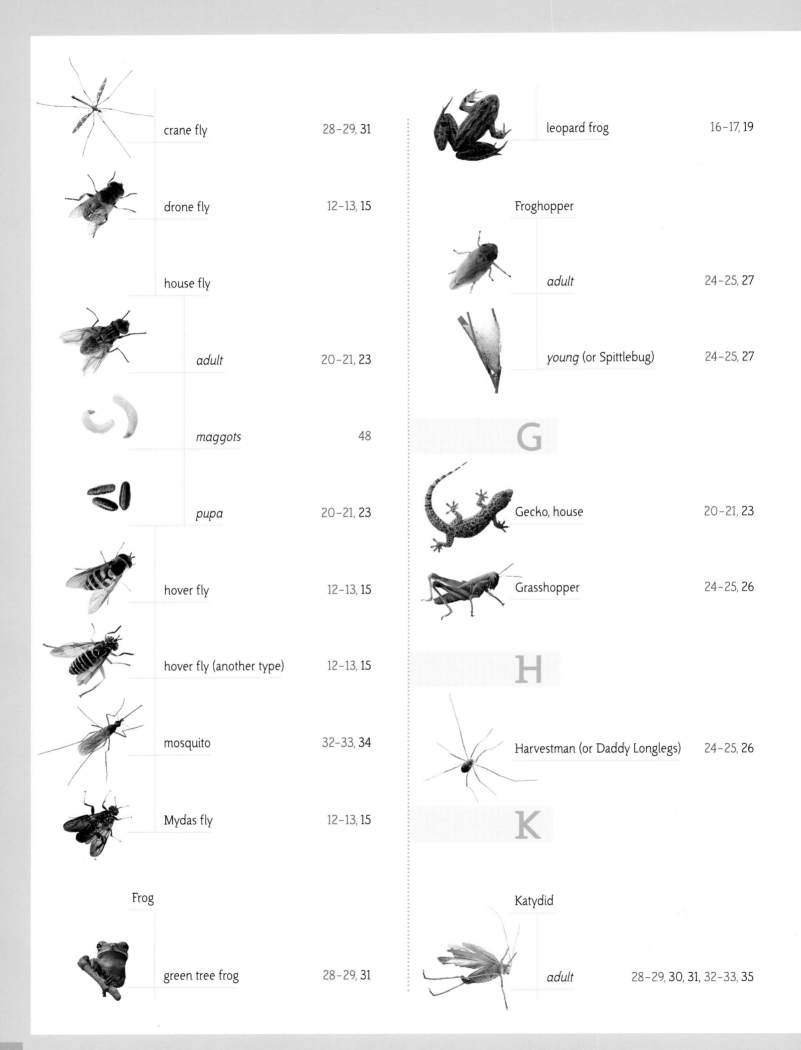

crane fly	28–29, 31	
drone fly	12–13, 15	
house fly		
adult	20–21, 23	
maggots	48	
pupa	20–21, 23	
hover fly	12–13, 15	
hover fly (another type)	12–13, 15	
mosquito	32–33, 34	
Mydas fly	12–13, 15	

Frog

green tree frog 28–29, 31

leopard frog 16–17, 19

Froghopper

adult 24–25, 27

young (or Spittlebug) 24–25, 27

G

Gecko, house 20–21, 23

Grasshopper 24–25, 26

H

Harvestman (or Daddy Longlegs) 24–25, 26

K

Katydid

adult 28–29, 30, 31, 32–33, 35

*Page numbers in purple refer to pictures. Page numbers in **black** refer to text.*

young   28–29, **31**

L

Lacewing   28–29, **30**, **32–33**, **35**

Ladybug beetle (see Beetle)

Leafhopper, scarlet and green   24–25, **27**

M

Milkweed bug (see Bug)

Millipede   8–9, **10**

Mite, red   8–9, **10**

Mole   8–9, **11**

Mosquito (see Fly)

Moth

cecropia moth

adult   48

caterpillar   28–29, **31**

caterpillars, young   28–29, **31**

cocoon   28–29, **31**

eggs   28–29, **31**

hornworm moth

adult   48

caterpillar   16–17, **18**

caterpillar, baby   16–17, **18**

eggs   16–17, **18**

*Page numbers in purple refer to pictures. Page numbers in **black** refer to text.*

45

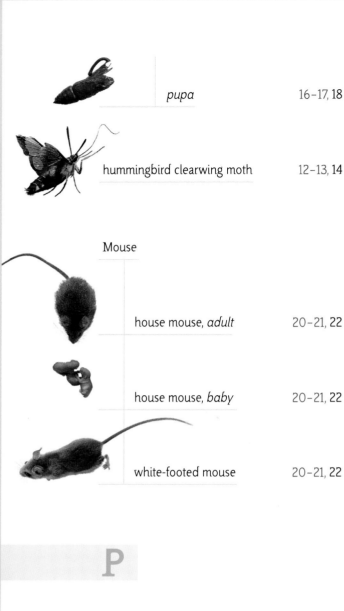

pupa	16–17, **18**
hummingbird clearwing moth	12–13, **14**

Mouse

house mouse, *adult*	20–21, **22**
house mouse, *baby*	20–21, **22**
white-footed mouse	20–21, **22**

Praying mantis

adult	28–29, **30**
egg case	28–29, **30**
young	28–29, **30**
Pseudoscorpion	8–9, **10**

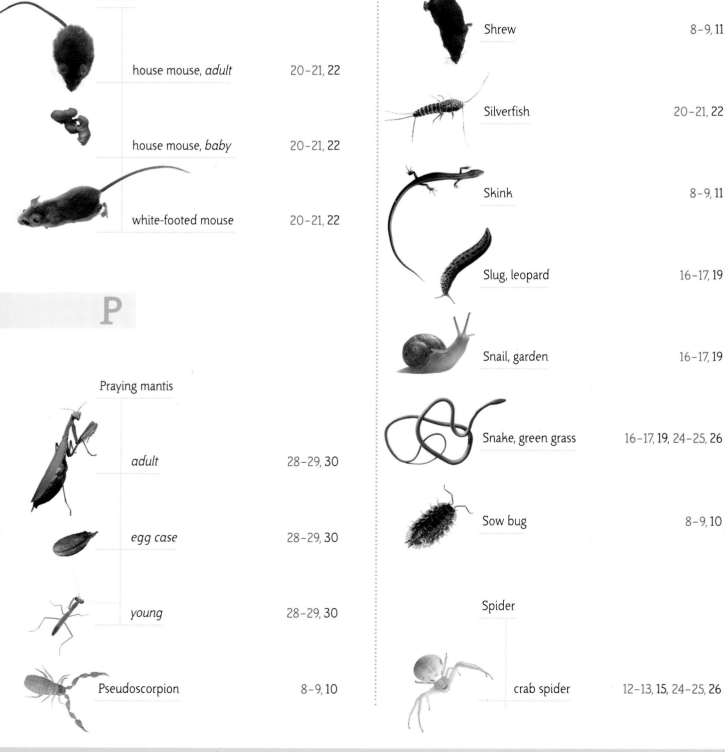

Salamander, redback	8–9, **11**
Shrew	8–9, **11**
Silverfish	20–21, **22**
Skink	8–9, **11**
Slug, leopard	16–17, **19**
Snail, garden	16–17, **19**
Snake, green grass	16–17, **19**, 24–25, **26**
Sow bug	8–9, **10**

Spider

crab spider	12–13, **15**, 24–25, **26**

*Page numbers in purple refer to pictures. Page numbers in **black** refer to text.*

T

W

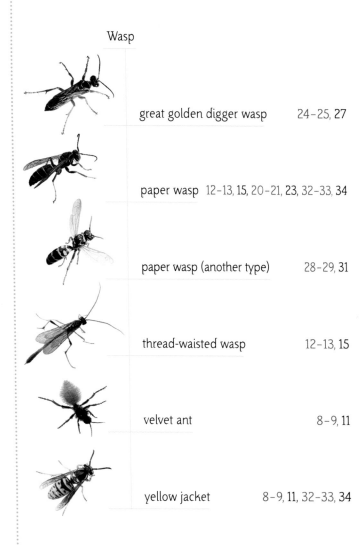

Y

Page numbers in purple refer to pictures. Page numbers in **black** *refer to text.*

47

cecropia moth

ABOUT THE PHOTOGRAPHS

Each large picture in this book is really made of more than sixty different photographs that have been combined to create a realistic illustration. The animals, and many of the plants and other items, were first photographed individually. Then they were scanned into a computer so they could be "cut out" and "pasted" together to build a single picture. Care had to be taken to make sure the final scenes were as true to life as possible. Each photograph was taken with the same lighting to help it look as if everything were photographed at the same time. The animals had to be cut out in the computer very precisely—even each tiny ant—and everything had to have its own shadow created. The flying and jumping animals were photographed using special techniques. To catch the action on film a sensitive laser trigger was used, which tripped a very fast shutter when the insect flew in front of the camera lens. Special high-speed strobes were used to freeze the insect in motion.

hornworm moth

ACKNOWLEDGMENTS

I wish to thank the following people for their help finding many of the animals in this book: Don Winans (Worcester EcoTarium), Lyle Jensen (New England Alive), Jane Winchell (Peabody Essex Museum), Greg Mertz (New England Wildlife Center), Joseph Merritt and Meade Cadot (Harris Center for Conservation Education), the Newport Butterfly Farm, the Massachusetts Audubon Society, Elissa Landre, Ron and Gay Munro, Audrey Bishop, and Inge and Arnie Weinberg. For her editorial comments, thanks to Lauren Thompson. I also wish to thank my wife for her good humor and wonderful patience in sharing the house with so many six-legged visitors over the years.

house fly maggots

Library of Congress Cataloging-in-Publication Data
Bishop, Nic, 1955- ❦ Backyard detective: critters up close / Nic Bishop. ❦ p.   cm. ❦ Summary: Describes a variety of animals and insects that can be found close to home and offers tips on how to observe them. ❦ ISBN 0-439-17478-3 ❦
1. Urban animals—Juvenile literature. [1. Animals. 2. Insects.] I. Title. ❦ QL49 .B62 2002 ❦ 591.75'6—dc21 ❦ 2001057620

10 9 8 7 6 5 4 3 2 1   02 03 04 05 06

Printed in Singapore   46
First edition, August 2002

Book design by Nancy Sabato
The text was set in Hattrick and Naomi.